Walking around Preston

by
Ian O. Brodie & Peter Davy

DALESMAN BOOKS
1972

35p.

THE DALESMAN PUBLISHING COMPANY LTD.,
CLAPHAM (via Lancaster), YORKSHIRE
First Published 1972

©   Ian O. Brodie and Peter Davy, 1972

ISBN : O 85206 160 9

Printed in Great Britain by
GEO. TODD & SON,
Marlborough Street, Whitehaven.

CONTENTS

		Page
Introduction		7

Circular Walks

Hutton — River Ribble — Grange Lane — Hutton	9
Penwortham Bridge — Howick — Penwortham	11
Bee Lane — Farington Moss — Whitestake — Bee Lane	13
Avenham — Brownedge — Walton — Avenham	14
Walton-le-Dale — Cuerdale — Walton	16
Higher Walton — Roach Bridge — Higher Walton	18
Five Barred Gate — Samlesbury — Spring Lane	20
Moor Nook — Lower Brockholes — Moor Nook	22
Moor Nook — Cow Hill — Ribbleton — Moor Nook	23
Grimsargh — Alston — Grimsargh	26
Grimsargh — Longridge — Grimsargh	28
Brookfield — Haighton — Brookfield	31
Tower Lane — Haighton — Pudding Pie Nook — Tower Lane	33
Broughton — Barton — Pudding Pie Nook — Broughton	35
Around Barton	38
Woodplumpton — Catforth — Woodplumpton ...	40
Ingol — Woodplumpton Brook — Lightfoot Green — Ingol	42
Ashton — Lea — Cottam — Ashton	45
Lea — Lea Town — Ashton — Lea	47
Scales — Treasles — Bolton Croft — Salwick — Scales	49

Sponsored Walks

Penwortham Bridge — River Ribble — Hutton — Lower Penwortham	52
Fulwood — Haighton — Goosnargh — Barton — Woodplumpton — Fulwood	55
Haslem Park — Woodplumpton — Cottam — Haslem Park	59
Log of Walks	62
The Country Code	64

ACKNOWLEDGMENTS

Authors alone can never claim all the credit for their book and we are no exception. Our thanks go to Miss Alma Kershaw for long hours of typing and valuable criticism, to Mr. W. S. McCubbin whose artistic skills bring life to the pages and finally to the pupils of Ashton-on-Ribble School who accompanied us unsuspectingly on many of the walks.

Maps by E. Gower.

The back cover sketch is of The Treales Windmill (see Walk 20).

INTRODUCTION

THE TRADITION of walking is very strong in the Preston area — it even manifests itself in the processions of the Guild Merchant. This tradition is not surprising when we consider the beautiful areas of the Lake District, the Yorkshire Dales and the Bowland Fells, all within easy reach of Preston. Much of this is real ramblers' country and often becomes too strenuous for all members of the family. However, the countryside in the immediate vicinity of the town provides walks of a less demanding nature. This area is very much tied up with the drainage pattern of the River Ribble, indeed several walks use the river bank or follow the Ribble Valley. The Lancaster canal is also a pleasant feature in a landscape of green fields, mature woods and isolated farmsteads.

Many people have noticed the increasing number of green footpath signs that have appeared recently. Beyond these signs pointing into the fields the rest of the footpath often remains a mystery. We hope this book will unravel some of these mysteries. The circular routes of between three and six miles, mostly on footpaths or quiet lanes, offer a pleasant afternoon or evening stroll of two or three hours' duration. The starting point of each walk is easily reached by local public transport. Details of this, along with car parking facilities, are given at the beginning of each walk description.

In recent years there has been an increase in the use of sponsored walks as a means of raising money. The popularity somewhat waned when a few accidents occurred on roads. We include three Sponsored Walk routes — mainly on footpaths — that could be used by safety-conscious walks organisers.

You don't really need a separate map to follow these routes — we hope the route plan and description are enough to see you safely round. However, there are a lot more footpaths to explore in the area, in spite of the fact that the twenty walks almost never cover the same path twice. Nevertheless we do recommend you to look over these routes on a 1in. Ordnance Survey (Sheet 94) map or better still on the 2½in. sheets.

It does sometimes occur that a farmer forgets a footpath crosses his land when he is placing barbed wire around fields or electric fences across them. We have endeavoured to make sure that any obstructions we found en route will have disappeared by the time you come round. If you do find an obstruction don't let it spoil your walk — find a way round it and notify the Rambler's Association, c/o 17 Stratford Drive, Fulwood, Preston, of where and when you found it. The canal towpath is not a public footpath. The British Waterways Board has no objection to you using the tow-paths but please respect other users — the anglers. Please notify the British Waterways Board, Lancaster, if you intend using Sponsored Walks B and C.

In following these walks you will cross many stiles and pass through many gates — remembering the Country Code. When a stile *is* a stile is a very debatable point. Some are just gaps between stones, others are no different from a low fence, yet others are more traditional with their cross piece. We haven't dared to define a stile for our route description — their variety is endless.

A word about footwear. Boots are not essential but after rain some of the lanes and farmyards can become very muddy. Be prepared.

1 HUTTON — RIVER RIBBLE — GRANGE LANE — HUTTON.

— 6½ miles —

Bus : *Ribble — Longton, Southport, Liverpool Services to Hutton Grammar School. Corporation — P5 to Anchor Inn terminus, then walk to Hutton Grammar School.*

Car : *Park by shops after Hutton Grammar School.*

OPPOSITE THE entrance to Hutton Grammar School is a short lane to a farm (footpath sign — Ratten Lane). Follow the lane into the farmyard, using the stiles if the gates are closed. Go through the yard to a stile and cross to follow the left-hand hedge to a gap in the corner. Pass through the gap and follow the right-hand fence and hedge through two fields to reach Ratten Lane by a short track at the side of a house. Turn left in Ratten Lane, and cross to the start of an enclosed path by the side of the bungalow "Belmont". Follow the path to the sub-station, then turn behind the bungalow to reach a stile in the far corner.

Over the stile follow the right-hand fence and hedge through two fields. Entering the third field by a stile, cross the field to aim for the left of three farms ahead. A sharp drop in the field leads to a stile over which you go to the bank of Mill Brook. Turn left and follow, with the brook on your right, the brookside path to reach, after a mile, the River Ribble. Turn left along the river bank, which you follow for almost two miles. This brings you to a small sewerage station and to where the embankment sweeps away from the river. Follow the embankment until a metal trough appears down on your left.

Cross the stile on the right of the trough and follow the left-hand fence to a gate at the end of Grange Lane. Go through the gate towards Old Grange Farm. Just short of

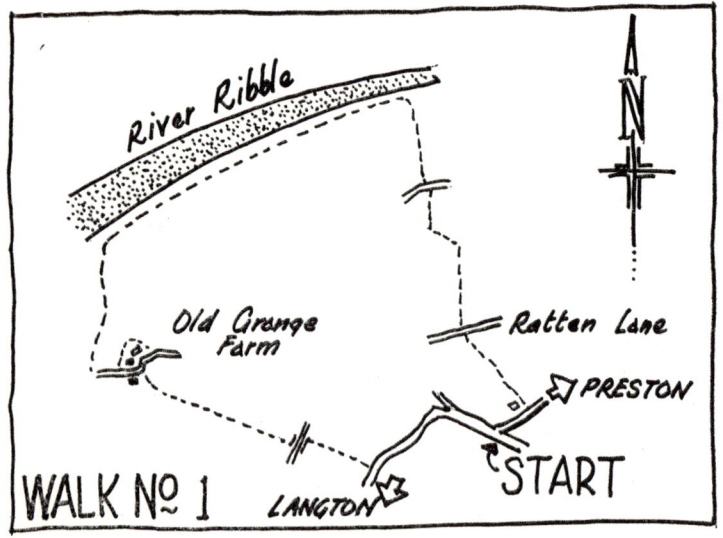

WALK Nº 1

the farm a gate on your left is opposite a gate on your right. Go through the former and follow the line of trees until you are opposite the edge of the farm buildings on the right. Turn right and skirt the buildings to reach a gate opposite a bungalow. Through this turn right on the road until you reach a gate on the left by a perched fuel tank. Go through the gate, keeping the farm houses on your right to pass to another gate.

Continue in the same direction along a right-hand hedge to reach a stile in the far right-hand corner of the field. From over this stile go diagonally left across the field to a stile over a ditch some threequarters of the way down the left-hand hedge. Cross the stile and aim for the pylon facing you to reach the next stile. Over this continue along the left-hand fence until a footbridge enables you to cross the stream, Longton Brook, on your right. Over the stream follow the bank until it takes you to the rear of some bungalows to a metalled road. Re-cross the stream and take the path that follows the other bank until this brings you to Liverpool Road. Turn left and a short walk will bring you back to your start.

2 PENWORTHAM BRIDGE — HOWICK — PENWORTHAM.

— 6 miles —

Bus : *Preston Corporation — Broadgate service to Penwortham Bridge.*

Car : *Park by riverside road to power station.*

FROM Penwortham Bridge follow the western bank (the Penwortham side) of the River Ribble downstream past the power station. Continue along the riverside track that passes opposite the entrance to Preston Dock, the Bull Nose, until you reach the second set of overhead supply lines. Between the last two pylons turn left down the track and follow it along to Marsh Farm and adjoining cottages. From here the track becomes a metalled road. Follow this, ignoring the right turn opposite Pollard's Farm, to reach Liverpool Road at Howick Cross.

Cross Liverpool Road to Howick Moor Lane, slightly to the right, and follow down the lane, continuing straight ahead when the metalled section ends (footpath sign — Broad Oak Lane). By the gate at the end a narrow path winds off to the left. This path, in a narrow wood, leads to the track of the disused Preston/Southport railway line.

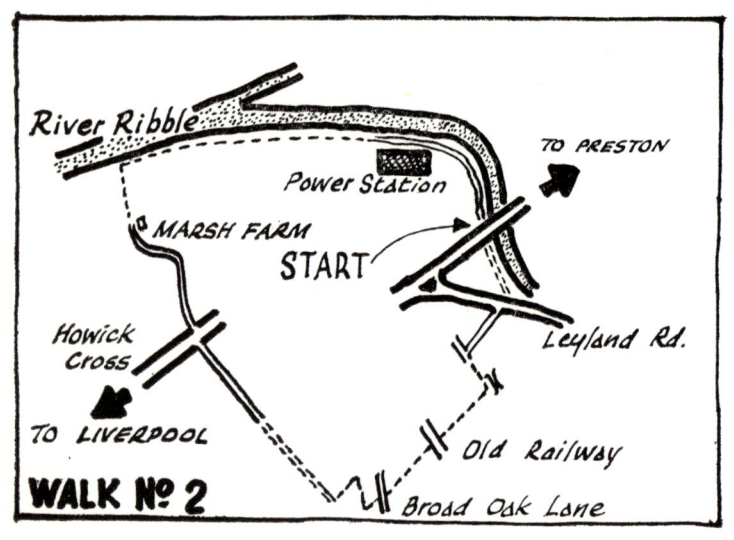

River Ribble

Power Station

TO PRESTON

MARSH FARM

START

Howick Cross

Leyland Rd.

TO LIVERPOOL

Old Railway

WALK Nº 2

Broad Oak Lane

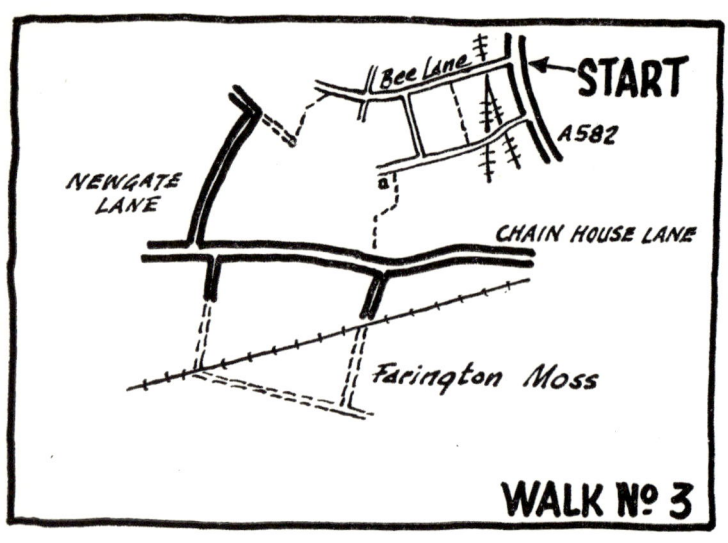

Bee Lane

START

A582

NEWGATE LANE

CHAIN HOUSE LANE

Farington Moss

WALK Nº 3

12

Turn left along this, going through the Broad Oak Lane level crossing and under two stone arched bridges to reach the metal bridge. Climb out from the cutting to the left of the bridge where there is a stile by a wooden fence. Cross this and follow the green path to a white gate and stile. Thirty yards after the stile turn right (Bridlepath sign) and follow the track down to Leyland Road. Turn right and cross the road, then go left along the river bank to reach Penwortham Bridge, with Penwortham Holme playing fields on your left.

---

3   BEE LANE — FARINGTON MOSS — WHITESTAKE — BEE LANE

— 5 miles —

Bus: *Ribble — Chorley via Leyland services to Bee Lane.*

Car: *Park in Bee Lane, off the Preston/Leyland Road, opposite Lostock Hall Gas Works.*

GO OVER THE railway bridge in Bee Lane and after the second lamp post on your left (opposite the house) is a gate and then a stile. Over the stile follow the right-hand hedge through two fields to emerge on a lane by a bungalow.
Turn right along the lane, going straight on when Lords Lane goes right, to reach the bungalow on the left. On the near side of the bungalow an enclosed path takes you left. Over the stile follow the left-hand hedge to the corner, continuing to follow the hedge as it swings right to pass through a gap between two trees.

Go left to cross the footbridge, and over this turn right to follow along the ditch. Over the next footbridge turn left to reach Chain House Lane between the bungalows and greenhouses, and then cross the road and go down Brook Lane (by the shop). Continue straight down onto the Moss, over the railway and by a level crossing to reach a white farm-house. After this, turn right at the T-junction of tracks, and go along until you reach the railway line again. Cross, and go down the track (Parker Lane), to reach once more Chain House Lane. Turn left, cross the road, then right into New-gate Lane. After the houses, continue along until the lane turns sharp left to become Green Lane.

Here turn right down the enclosed track until it opens into a field; do not enter the field facing you but the one on your left. Go along the right-hand hedge and ditch in this field to reach a footbridge. Cross this and then follow the left-hand hedge, passing a pit, to reach the left-hand side of a farm. Follow the track which starts on the left of the farm and then passes round to the right to join the lane that leads you into Bee Lane and your start.

---

4 AVENHAM — BROWNEDGE — WALTON — AVENHAM.

— 5½ miles —

Avenham Park — Tram Bridge.

CROSS Tram Bridge and follow the tree-lined walk for over a mile until it rises, then bear left to reach Brownedge Road. Cross straight over to a stile (footpath sign) and again follow the enclosed lane to reach Todd Lane North. At the lane turn right downhill and, just before the housing starts, cross the road to a farm track (footpath sign — Brownedge Road), which you follow to the farm. Go through the farmyard and, in the corner to the right of two gates, go to cross the stile. Follow the right-hand hedge to another stile.

Cross this stile and turn left up a fenced path — to the rear of bungalows and houses on your right-hand side. When the path enters a field continue in the same direction—with a

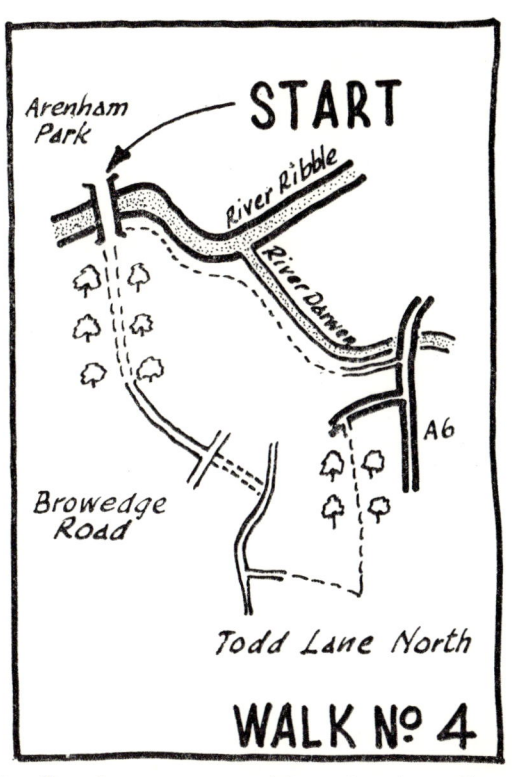

START

Arenham Park

River Ribble

River Darwen

A6

Browedge Road

Todd Lane North

WALK Nº 4

wooded valley down on your right. Another stile takes the path into the wood. Continue through the wood and when it ends look for a stile in the top left-hand corner. Cross this and go down by the houses to Wateringpool Lane/Todd Lane, where turn right and go downhill to reach the A6.

Turn left by the garage and go down the A6 until Walton Green turns off on the left. Go down this quaint lane, continuing past the farm (the River Darwen on the right) to reach the bank of the River Ribble. Follow the path along the river bank to the Tram Bridge and retrace your steps into Avenham Park.

15

Bus : Ribble — Gregson Lane or Rochdale services to Knot Lane.

Car : Park in Knot Lane, off Blackburn Old Road, Walton-le-Dale.

GO DOWN Knot Lane to the Blackburn Road and cross to a footpath (footpath sign — Chorley Road). Go along, cross the footbridge and take the path to the left along the river. The path goes up the bank (known locally as "Forty Steps"), then along the left-hand hedge to the farm. Go to the farm road through the yard, and follow it to where it bends right. Here carry straight on over a stile by a gate and follow the left-hand hedge to reach the edge of the concrete works. The enclosed path goes to reach School Lane.

Turn left along School Lane, go over the motorway bridge, then cross School Lane to go down a track by the motorway in front of the cottage. Follow the track round and turn left at the junction. After 100 yards go left to a stile by a five-barred gate as the track you have just left goes down and round to a farm. Over the stile follow the left-hand hedge round and down to a gate to rejoin School Lane. Turn right, then left at the junction with Blackburn Road by the shop.

Over the bridge, cross the road and turn right into Shop Lane, then left into Bannister Hall Lane (footpath sign — Potter Lane). At the end of the estate cross the cattle grid and turn left to follow a rising track to reach two adjacent gates. Cross the stile on the right of the right-hand gate and follow the right-hand hedge to the top corner of the field. Cross here, opposite the farm house, and go along to a gate on the left. This leads into the farmyard; enter but leave

16

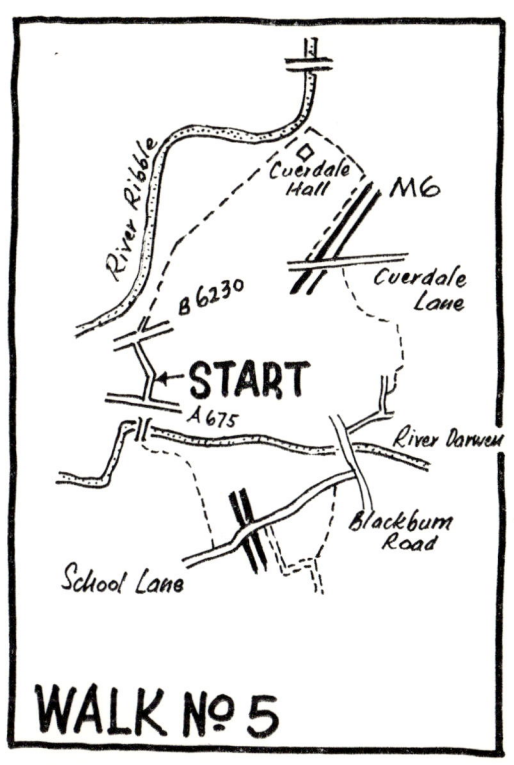

WALK № 5

it immediately by the gate on your right. In the field, cross the middle (diagonally to the right) to reach a gateway in the far corner. Through the gate follow the right-hand hedge to a double stile, ten yards to the left of the corner, which you cross. Go diagonally left towards a white rail fence to cross a stile in a new fence. Continue to a gateway in the left-hand corner of the next field, after which the right-hand hedge leads to Cuerdale Lane, reached by a stile and a gate.

Turn left over the motorway bridge, cross the road, then turn right over a stile (footpath sign — Brockholes Bridge).

Follow the right-hand hedge/fence that keeps you above the motorway; this path continues to a stile where the motorway emerges from the cutting overlooking the Ribble Valley. Here turn left and follow the left-hand hedge to a gate, then go to reach the right-hand side of Cuerdale Hall Farm just by the River Ribble. Go left round the farm to a gate near the river, and through this follow the left-hand wall to a gate and stile.

Cross and continue in the same direction along the left-hand fence and hedge to reach a stile by a notice in the far left-hand corner of the field. Over this again take the left-hand hedge to a gateway, through here following the left-hand hedge to reach the river bank. Go left to reach Ribble Side Farm — the farm track leads up to Knot Lane and your start.

---

6   HIGHER WALTON — ROACH BRIDGE — HIGHER WALTON

— 5 miles —

Bus : Ribble — Rochdale service to Old Oak Hotel.

Car : Park in Fox Lane, off Blackburn Old Road.

FROM THE SIDE of the Old Oak Hotel on the Blackburn Old Road, go along Fox Lane and continue as it bends right after the houses, ignoring the footpath sign on the left (Houghton Lane) to reach just short of the farm house. Here a stile on the right is crossed; then follow the left-hand hedge past the farm house until just short of the corner of the field. On your left a stone slab footbridge and stile should be crossed. Over here turn right to follow the right-hand hedge until you are thirty yards past a gap made by a hedge coming up from your left. Turn sharp left to go down parallel to this hedge to reach a stile.

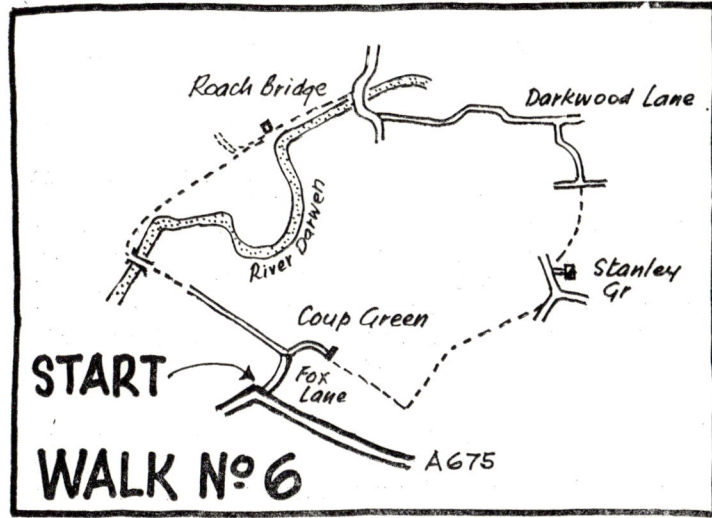

Roach Bridge

Darkwood Lane

River Darwen

Stanley Gr

Coup Green

START →

Fox Lane

WALK Nº 6

A675

Cross this and follow the left-hand hedge over the field to the top of a wood. Go slightly right and down to cross Quaker Brook by a wooden footbridge. Climb the opposite bank by the left-hand fence/hedge to reach a wicket gate on the right of a stone built house. Through this turn left along the road and left again at the junction by Stanley Grange.

Cross to the right-hand side, and at the end of the brick wall a short gated lane (footpath sign — Firwood Lane) leads you towards the wooden buildings of the Police Training School.

On your left, behind the house, a stile leads you into a sloping field. Go right, away from the road, and down to reach two adjacent gates. Go through the second of these (the first leads into a field containing football goal posts) to follow the left-hand fence/hedge. Thirty yards to the right of the corner is a stile. Cross and follow the hedge line (on your right) across the field to the remains of a footbridge.

19

Cross here and climb to a stile, and again follow the right-hand hedge to a stile by a gate. Turn right on the road, then immediately left down Darkwood Lane.

Follow this until it turns right and a farm lane goes left (footpath sign — Roach Bridge). Follow this farm 'cul-de-sac" to reach Cardwell's Farm, and continue through the yard on the concrete track which eventually becomes a green lane. This, followed through two gates, leads down to Roach Bridge paper mill where a stile leads on to the road. Turn right, past the mill, to cross the bridge and then turn left (footpath sign — Cuerdale Lane, Carver Bridge). Go between the cottages and garages to a stile tucked in the left-hand corner behind the cottages.

Follow the river bank, keeping below the farm, to reach a farm road. Go along this until it bends right, where go straight on through a gate to cross a field and regain the river bank by a stile. Continue past Red Rock Falls to a tubular footbridge (footpath sign — Hoghton Lane). Cross this and follow the path that becomes a lane; this leads to Coup Green and then Fox Lane — your starting point.

---

7   **FIVE BARRED GATE — SAMLESBURY**
— SPRING LANE.

— 4½ miles —

Bus : Ribble — Blackburn New Road services to Five Barred Gate Hotel.

Car : Park by the Five Barred Gate Hotel.

ENTER THE FIELD adjacent to the Preston side of the Five Barred Gate Hotel by a concrete stile next to a gate. Follow the right-hand hedge to reach a stile in the further-most corner of the field — in line with the house and petrol station. Over the stile follow the left-hand fence to a stile

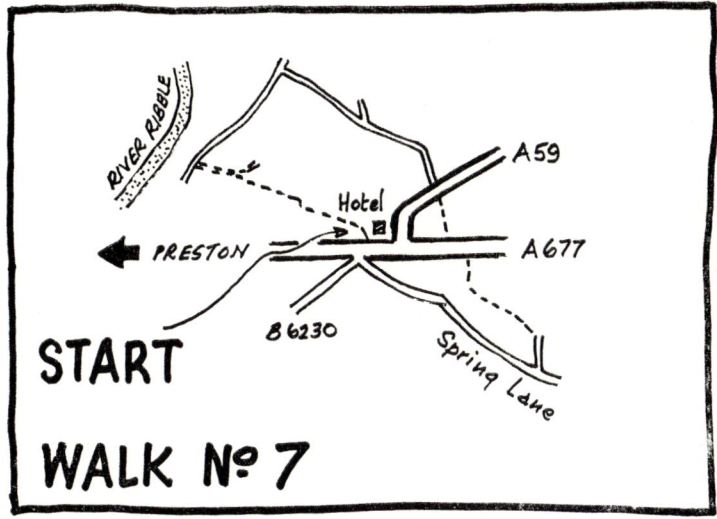

START

WALK № 7

and gateway. Over this stile turn right and follow the right-hand hedge through two fields to a gate. Then follow the path down the field, heading in the direction of Coultauld's chimneys. Continue down on the track you meet until it enters a metalled lane, turning right along this to reach a white farmhouse.

Just after the farm leave the metalled road by turning right onto a farm track that climbs besides a stream, going past two small farm bungalows until the track again becomes metalled. Just after this, on a bend, turn right to follow the green lane over the stream and continue to reach the A59. Cross straight over to a stile by a gate and follow the left-hand hedge to another stile to reach the Blackburn New Road. Turn left and cross to a gate and footpath sign — Spring Lane. Go through the gate, labelled "Hermitage," then pass through a swing gate and follow the cobbled path down to a bridge over the stream by the "Hermitage." Cross the bridge to a stile on the right, going through this to climb

to the right to another stile. Over this turn left and follow
the left-hand hedge through two long fields to reach a stile.

Over the stile continue to follow the left-hand fence until
a stile is reached half way along. Cross, turn right and
follow the fence to a gate. Go right through the gate and
follow the enclosed lane, by the site of the old sewerage
works, to reach Spring Lane. Turn right and go along this
quiet lane to the Five Barred Gate Hotel.

8   MOOR NOOK — LOWER BROCKHOLES — MOOR NOOK.

— 3 miles —

Bus : Corporation — Moor Nook service to terminus.

*Car : Park at the end of Pope Lane where Grange Park meets
the Motorway.*

FROM THE bus terminus go right down Grisedale Cres-
cent, turn left into Marl Hill Crescent and again left into
Greenthorn Crescent — all the time with views over the
Ribble Valley. Just before Parlick Road leaves Greenthorn
Crescent a path goes left (by a telegraph pole) between trees
and shrubs. This distinct path leads down steeply through
Brockholes Wood to reach a stile on the left at the bottom
edge of the wood.

Cross and follow the left-hand hedge to reach the side of
Lower Brockholes Farm. Join the farm track and go right,
past the farm house, to reach the junction just above the
river. Turn left and follow this track under the motorway,
eventually reaching Higher Brockholes Farm. Keeping to
the right of the farmhouse the path leads through the yard
towards Bolton Wood. Ignore the track that goes off to the
right and take the stile leading into the wood. Bearing
slightly left the path climbs up through the wood to reach

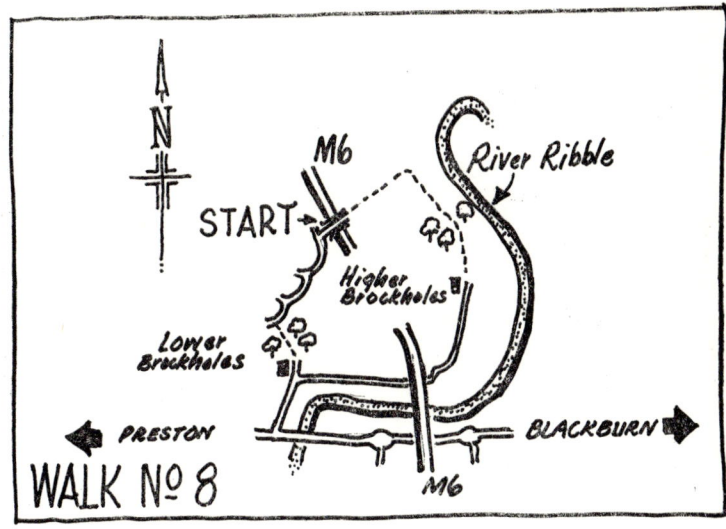

WALK Nº 8

Grange Park. Follow the left-hand hedge of the park along the wood to reach the motorway, and just to your right, over the motorway bridge, your start.

---

9 MOOR NOOK — COW HILL — RIBBLETON — MOOR NOOK.

— 5 miles —

Bus: Corporation — Moor Nook services to terminus.

Car: Park at the end of Pope Lane where Grange Park meets the motorway.

LEAVE Moor Nook to cross the motorway bridge and enter Grange Park, continuing along the left-hand side of the Park to reach the far corner and a gap in the hedge. Through

23

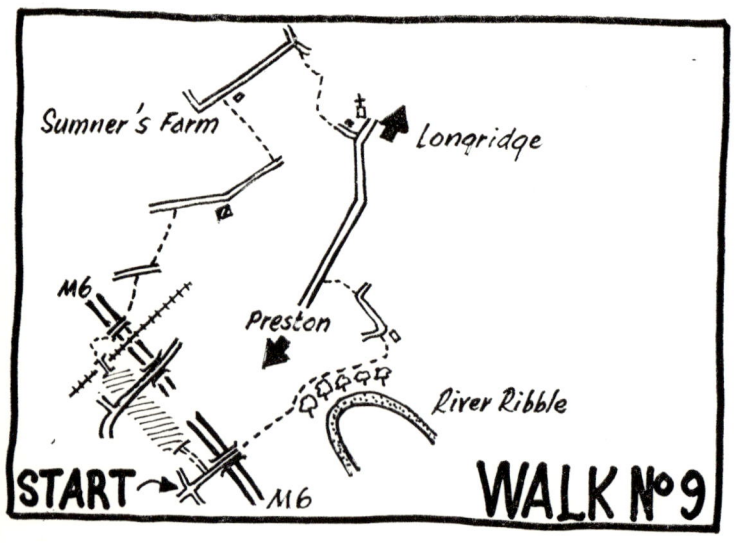

here, on your left is a stile. Cross and follow the cindered path along the top edge of the wood until it bears left to reach the left-hand side of Tun Brook Head Farm. After a couple of stiles you emerge on the farm access road to your right — follow it as it turns left.

Continue along this farm road to where it turns right before Roman Road Farm. Leave the road to a stile and a cindered footpath, between fences, to reach Longridge Road. Turn right, to reach Three Mile Cross on your right (just past the Saint John Southworth School on your left).

Cross the road and continue to a white gate just short of Grimsargh church (footpath sign — Cow Hill). Go through the white gate down to Church House Farm and straight on between the buildings to a stile (stone steps) in the wall facing you. Cross it and continue in the same direction over the old railway bridge to another stile.

24

Cross this and head for the bottom right-hand corner of the field. Here a stone footbridge in the shrubs and a stile lead into the next field. Follow the left-hand hedge until you reach a stile and footbridge on your left (opposite the church up on your right). Go across this field to a stile towards the right-hand corner, and once over it aim for the left of the farm (Goose Hall) to reach the farm track. This leads you to a metalled road on which you turn left and follow to Sumner's Farm on your left.

After the wall, past the farm, there is a white gate on your left. Through here follow the track past the hen cabins and go straight to reach a gate in the hedge that runs at right angles to your path. Through the gate turn right in this short enclosed lane and continue along the left-hand hedge in the next field to reach Rough Hey Farm. Enter the yard by a gate and keep right to pass the farm house and go down the farm access road. Before the next farm is reached there is a pit on your right. Opposite this go left over a stile (in a state of disrepair) and follow the left-hand hedge towards the corner of the field.

Five yards short of the corner a stile on your left is crossed. Then turn right to follow the right-hand ditch to reach the right-hand corner of the field. Cross here to reach an enclosed lane, which you follow round to a stile by a gate on your left. Over the stile go to the right-hand hedge which you follow down to the motorway. Cross the motorway footbridge and after twenty yards an enclosed path starts on your right. Follow this, going away from the motorway and crossing the playing field to reach the railway line. Go over this by the footbridge ahead to come to the road.

Cross, go down Franklands Drive and then right via Glen Grove to reach the Longridge Road. (Those by bus can reach the Gammul Lane terminus to the right). Turn left, cross and go down the path between houses numbered 128 and 132. This leads to Alder Road which you follow to the far end; here turn right into Fir Trees Avenue and immediately cross to enter Grange Park on your left. By keeping to the motorway side you will rejoin your starting point.

Bus : *Longridge services to Elston Lane, Grimsargh.*

Car : *Park in Elston Lane (on your right after passing through Grimsargh).*

GO DOWN Elston Lane to a stile in the hedge on the left opposite bungalow Number 14. Cross the field slightly to your right to a stile by a beech tree, then skirt round the wood on the right until you are on a level with the house called "The Hermitage." Follow the line of trees left across the field towards the next farm, to meet a stile by a gate. Cross the stile, do not enter the yard of the farm, but cross to another stile (footpath sign — Ribchester via Alston). Follow the left-hand hedge, passing the farm buildings, towards the far corner of the field.

Just before the corner you will find a footbridge, down to the right. Cross and then go to a stile just up from the bridge. Over the stile follow the right-hand hedge to the top corner of the field. Turn left here and again follow the hedge on your right (i.e. in the same field) to reach a gate by a pit in the far corner. Through the gate continue along the right-hand hedge to a stile just short of the right-hand corner. Cross the stile and then follow the left-hand fence/hedge down the long field, crossing in the corner and turning to a stile and footbridge immediately on your left.

Over these make for the left-hand side of the cottages ahead, passing an old pit to reach a gate and short lane that leads onto the road by the cottages. Turn right and follow the lane down, passing the Observatory, to come to a right-hand turn to Alston Old Hall Farm. Go down this and where it leads right, just in front of the farm, turn left down a gated track to reach the metalled road just short of Boot

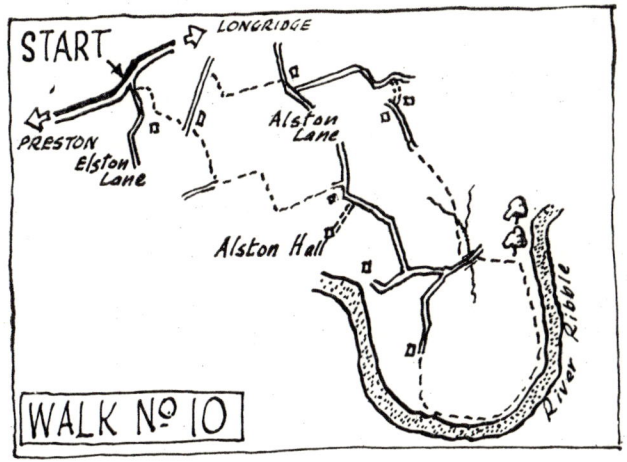

START

LONGRIDGE

PRESTON

Elston Lane

Alston Lane

Alston Hall

River Ribble

WALK Nº 10

Farm. Turn right and keep Boot Farm to your right as you pass through a gate, go down a track and pass over a stream to cross a stile by a white gate. The enclosed path then leads to the river bank.

Follow the bank of the Ribble round the large meander until it is crossed by a fence line which marks the start of a riverside wood. Cross the fence and start to climb the edge of the field keeping the wood on your right. Cross into the second field and continue until you are level with the cottages. Go left across the field, passing a pit on your left to reach the corner of the field. Go onto the farm access road, turn left to pass the farm cottages and reach a bridge.

Just over the bridge enter the field to your right, and go up the field keeping the trees on your right. The field dips down to a small stream where you will find a stile under an oak tree. Cross the stream and stile, and turn left in the next field to go up to a hedge line that comes down from the right. Go to the far side of this hedge and follow it up the field to reach the top right-hand corner. Cross in the corner and continue up the next field — again by the right-hand hedge — to meet a gate some forty yards to the left of the top corner. Through the gate follow the enclosed lane to the farm. Go through the yard and as you leave it, by a white gate, turn right to follow a track. When this track meets another track go left and follow this farm lane until it reaches Alston Lane.

Go right along the lane to cross a stile by a gate on the left — opposite the entrance to Hatherley Brake House on the right. Follow the right-hand hedge until near the far end of the field; after a red gate there is a stile by a black gate on your right. Cross the stile and follow the right-hand hedge to a stile and gate in the corner. Cross the stile, turn left and then go down the metalled road to the farm. Do not enter the farmyard but where the metalled track ends go to a stile and gate on the right. From here re-trace your steps past "The Hermitage" to reach Elston Lane.

11 GRIMSARGH — LONGRIDGE — GRIMSARGH

— 6 miles —

Bus: *Ribble — Longridge, Ribchester, Chipping services to Grimsargh Post Office.*

Car: *Park by Plough Inn.*

STARTING FROM the Plough Inn the enclosed path follows the side of the old railway line to Longridge until a fence crosses your way. Cross the stile in the corner, to your right, and then make for the left-hand corner of the reservoir. Here you join the farm track that takes you to Dam House Farm. Keep the farm to your right to reach two field gates. On your left before the gates is a fence;

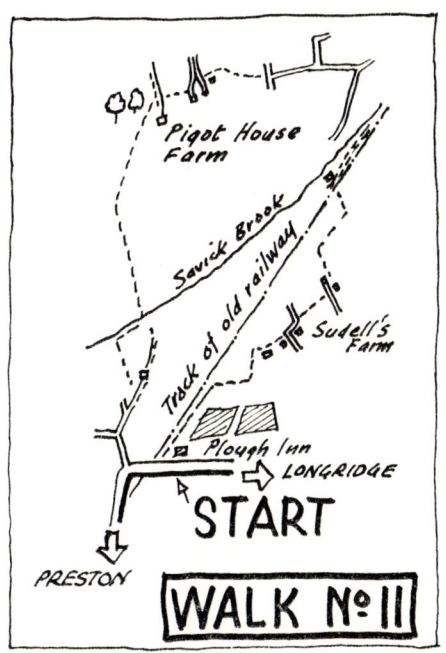

Piqot House Farm

Savick Brook

Track of old railway

Sudell's Farm

Plough Inn

⇨ LONGRIDGE

START

PRESTON

WALK Nº 11

cross here and follow the right-hand hedge to reach the next farm. Keep the farm on your right, go behind the wooden cabin and along the block wall to enter the yard of Sudell's Farm. Keep the farmyard on your right and start down the lane. Go through the first gate on your right and follow the left-hand hedge for twenty/thirty yards to a stile. Cross the stile, turn right and follow the ditch along to Hothersall Tenement Farm.

Go into the yard and turn left past the barn on the left. Go down the middle of the field to find a plank footbridge and stile about twenty yards from the far right-hand corner of the field. Cross these, turn right and continue across the field parallel to the railway, heading for the pylon and Long-ridge ahead. This leads you to a gate by a pit. Through the gate go towards the gate in front of the asbestos roof of Shaw Farm. The stile by the gate takes you over the rail-way track and then you can go to the left of the farm to enable you to turn into the farmyard.

Go through the yard and turn left into the lane starting behind the farmhouse. Follow this lane until it passes under the overhead transmission lines. Leave it here to follow the brook side to reach a stile and stepping stones and then another farm lane. Turn right in this lane and take the first lane on the left just through a gateway. Continue to follow this enclosed lane until it ends in a T-junction. Enter the field facing you and cross the middle to reach an obvious stile in the far hedge.

Over the stile follow the right-hand hedge until it brings you to a double stile opposite a farm house. Cross these and then follow the left-hand hedge to a stile, over which continue so as to join the farm lane. Go to the right on the lane until there is a stile on your left by a telegraph post, where cross and turn left up the parallel farm lane. Just before the farmyard turn right and go to the end of the farm buildings and the gate to enter the field above the stream. Continue to the far end and twenty yards above the corner cross into the drive to the white-painted Pigot House Farm.

The lane up to the farm is gated. Turn right by the gate to follow the stone wall on your left to another gate. Go through this and make for the left-hand corner of a small wood. Continue along the top of the wood and at the far side make for the right-hand of two gates up on your left. Cross the stile by this gate and follow the right-hand hedge to a gate in the corner. This leads into a scrap yard. Go straight across and again follow the right-hand hedge to the next corner (behind Harrison's Farm). Go across in the corner, turn left, and follow the left-hand hedge to a stile in the far left-hand corner of the field.

Over this go down the field to reach a footbridge in the bottom right-hand corner, crossing it to turn right and follow the stream. Cross the stile over the fence by the line of the old Whittingham railway line and then go across to a footbridge hidden by the slope of the land. Over the bridge follow the right-hand hedge towards the farm. Ignore the first stile in the hedge but go to a stile in the corner of the field behind the barn. Over this again follow the right-hand hedge to reach the farm access road. Follow this to the right to reach Grimsargh.

---

12 BROOKFIELD — HAIGHTON — BROOKFIELD

— 4½ miles —

Bus : Corporation — Brookfield services to top of Cromwell Road.

Car : Park Watling Street Road/Cromwell Road.

MOSSDALE Avenue leads off from Watling Street Road near to Cromwell Road. Follow the path down the Avenue, through "Hills and Hollows" to emerge on Longsands Lane. Turn left and follow the lane to the Continuation Hospital, where turn right and go down Midgery Lane to the bridge. Here, over the bridge, turn right up the steep farm road, passing Hindley Hill Farm on the left, to reach Hindley House Farm. Incline right as you enter the farmyard and go by the side of the farm buildings to join the fields by a gate. From here you will see a footbridge which carries the footpath over the motorway. To reach it keep to the left-hand hedge until you are opposite the bridge.

Enter the field at the other side of the bridge, bear left and after a few yards look for a stile on the right (by a corner in the adjacent field). Cross and follow the left-hand hedge to join a lane by Ladywell House. Go right down the lane, passing St. Mary's Well on the left to reach the metalled road

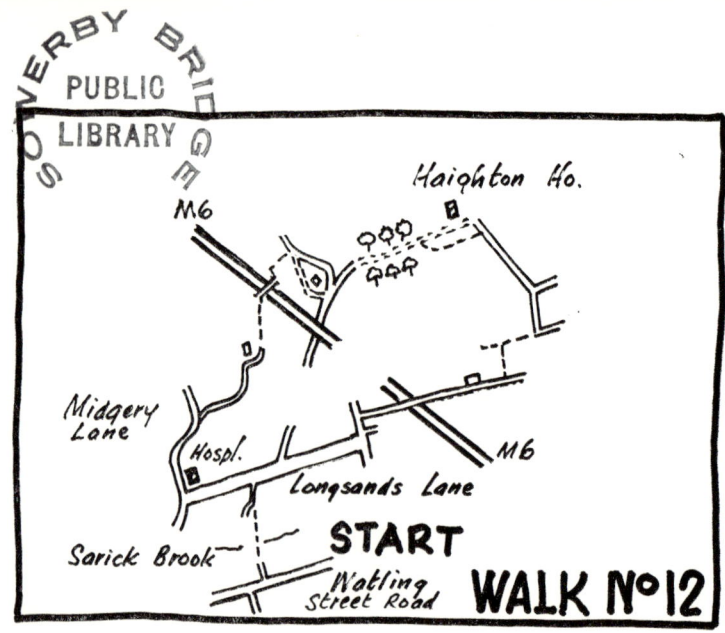

Haighton Ho.

M6

Midgery Lane

Hospl.

M6

Longsands Lane

Sarick Brook

START

Watling Street Road

WALK Nº 12

before the motorway bridge. Turn left and then pass through the gateway on the right to the private grounds of Haighton House, often known as "Bluebell Wood." Follow the driveway along until a footbridge crosses the stream on the right. Cross this and follow the lower path with the stream on your left to reach Londonderry Bridge and the metalled road.

Turn right up the road, ignoring the first turn left, until you reach the left-hand bend in the road. Cross the stile in the right-hand corner and then the other stile just a bit further along. Continue along the left-hand hedge to reach a stile by a gateway in the field corner. Cross this and follow the hedge round left to another stile in the corner of the field. Cross, and continue along the left-hand hedge to reach a gate by a tree.

Go through the gap and again follow the line of the left-hand hedge, this time to reach a gate. Through the gate follow the farm access road to the right through the farm-

32

yard and over the motorway bridge to reach a lane. Turn left and then right into Longsands Lane, and go along until you reach Fernyhalgh Lane on the right. Go left and retrace your steps over the "Hills and Hollows" (footpath sign — Watling Street Road).

---

13 TOWER LANE — HAIGHTON — PUDDING PIE NOOK — TOWER LANE.

— 5½ miles —

Bus : P2 service to Black Bull Lane.

Car : Park in Tower Lane, off Sharoe Green Lane North.

IF YOU GO by bus to the Black Bull, cross the Garstang Road and go down Sharoe Green Lane North and then left into Tower Lane. At its end continue along the farm track until it turns left — opposite you is a stile by a gate which you cross. Go diagonally left across the field to a foot-bridge, over which turn right and follow the brook to a stile. Cross and continue in the same direction with the brook and "Cromwell's Mound" on your right.

Keep right of the farm to reach a stile by a gate and foot-path sign. Turn right into Midgery Lane and just before the second gate on the left a high stile (footpath sign — Fernyhalgh Lane) is to be crossed. Follow the right-hand hedge to reach a stile in the corner by the motorway. Cross and follow the motorway over stiles and footbridge until you reach some steps that lead to a farm access bridge which crosses the motorway.

Go over this bridge and then down to a stile on the right of the left-hand of three gates. Cross this and go parallel to the motorway until you are half-way across the field. Here turn sharp right to reach a footbridge and stile.

33

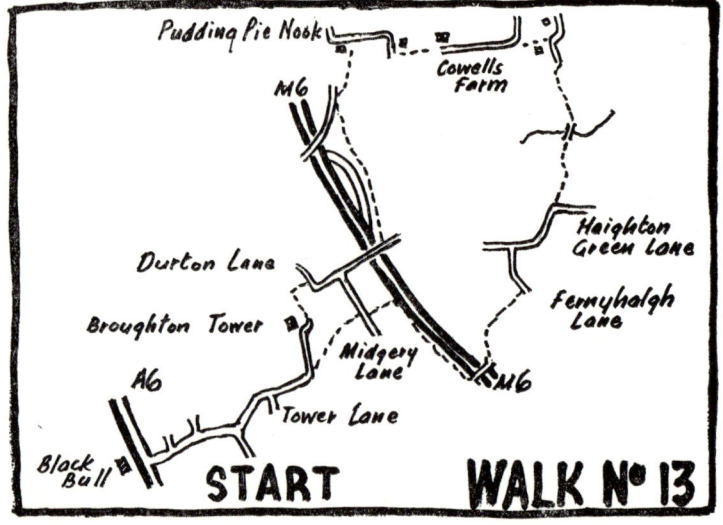

Cross these and follow the right-hand hedge through two fields to reach Fernyhalgh Lane by a gate to the right of the house. Turn left to reach the road junction and then right into Haighton Green Lane.

After the left and right-hand bends a stile on the left (footpath sign — Whittingham Lane) is reached just short of Fern Cottage. Cross and go to a stile in the far right hand corner of the field. Follow the right-hand hedge down through two fields to a footbridge over Blundell Brook. Continue up the field facing you, through a gap in the hedge, to the right-hand side of a depression. From here follow the farm track that bends round the pit until it comes to cross a ditch. On your right is a double stile; over it, follow the left-hand hedge and then the lane.

When the lane turns right to join a farmyard, go left over a stile by a gate and then across the field to the yard of Cowells Farm (via a feed hopper). Continue straight past the farm house and then take the farm lane to your left

34

when passing the gateway. Continue past the next farm on your left to the second gateway after it. Here is a stile and a white arrow. Follow the right-hand hedge, adjacent to the farm lane, past two stiles in front of New Field Farm and continue along the hedge to another stile.

Over this make for the left-hand side of the farm buildings ahead (Brook House). Go into the yard of the farm and then follow the access road round to the left to reach Pudding Pie Nook. When this road turns right you should turn left, past the side of the thatched cottage, to reach a gate. Enter the field and follow the left-hand hedge/fence through two fields. Go through the gateway to the side of the motorway.

Follow the motorway fence, with magnificent views of the bridge. Eventually this path becomes enclosed as it follows the motorway to Durton Lane. Here turn right over the motorway bridge, continue past Midgery Lane on your left and Winders Farm on your right, to where Durton Lane bends left. On your left is a gate (opposite the right-hand drive). Through here follow the left-hand hedge to a gate. Through this turn left to follow the lane to Broughton Tower Farm, and then by the farm access road to Tower Lane.

---

14 BROUGHTON — BARTON — PUDDING PIE NOOK — BROUGHTON.

— 5 miles —

Bus: *Ribble — Garstang and Morecambe services to Broughton Church.*

Car: *Park at the side of Broughton Church.*

FROM THE SIDE of Broughton church go along the right-hand edge of the school-yard to the far end. On your right is a stile by a double gate; over the stile follow the enclosed climb the field to a stile in the top right-hand corner, and to the right of a pit. Continue diagonally to a gap in the top far corner of the next field, by a concrete trough. From here take the side of the left-hand hedge to a double stile and again the left-hand hedge to a stile by a tree in the far left-hand corner. All this time you are heading for a white farmhouse (Yates) and the Orchard Restaurant.

Again follow round to the far left-hand corner to reach a stile, and then turn left along the lane towards the farm (Yates). Go round the front of the farm, then left down the metalled road to reach Whittingham Lane near the motorway bridge. Turn left along the lane, cross and go past the houses on your right to the farm. Turn into the yard and follow the lane that leads you past Hooles and Tunsteads Farm to just short of Three Stiles Cottages, where the lane bears left.

On your right is a stile between two gates. Cross and follow the left-hand hedge to a stile and the footbridge over the motorway. Cross the bridge and on the far side cross the stile on the left. Turn your back to the motorway and follow the right-hand hedge to a gap. Turn right through this and again go along the right-hand hedge/fence to a stile in the corner of the field. Over this, the right-hand hedge is followed as far as a metal gate just short of a pit.

Go through the gate and turn left down the enclosed lane that reaches a junction to the right of Barton House Farm. Turn right and follow the green lane down and round to Langley Lane. Turn right, cross and go left down a short lane, with a white, detached house on the corner, to reach Whittingham Lane. Again turn right, cross and go left, this time by Dean Farm (footpath sign — Pudding Pie Nook, Haighton Green Lane). Follow this along to Pudding Pie Nook and turn right immediately after the thatched Cardwells Cottage. Go down the side of the cottage to enter the field by a gate.

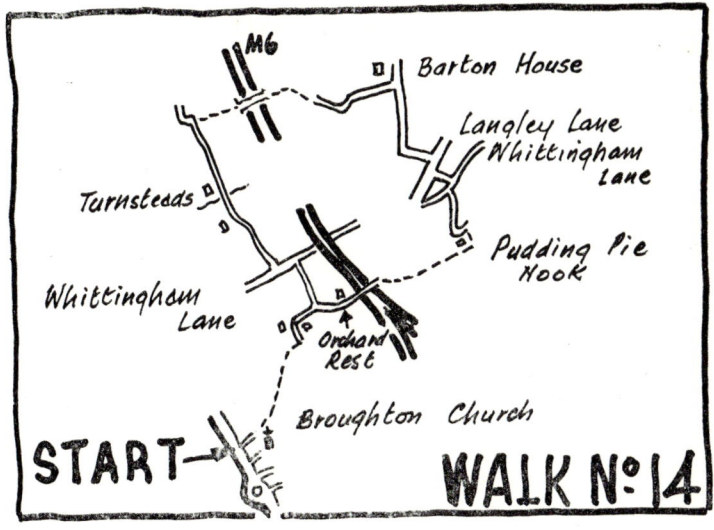

Through the gate turn right to follow the ditch and hedge to reach a stile in the corner. Cross and continue in the path until it ends in another stile. From here turn left to same direction to the motorway. Cross the footbridge and join the road in front of the Orchard Restaurant, going along the drive to reach the far side of the white Yates Farm. From here your steps can be retraced to Broughton by going down the lane past the farm to a stile on your right. Cross this and go past the lone tree in the field to the next stile. From here follow the right-hand hedge through three fields before going down through two fields to the enclosed path — the whole time aiming for the tower of Broughton church.

Bus : *Ribble — Garstang and Morecambe services to Kopper Kettle.*

Car : *Park in Thorntrees Avenue, off the A6, just past Barton Hall.*

CROSS THE A6, go down Thorntrees Avenue to Woodland Way, and facing you (between houses 8 and 10) is an enclosed footpath (footpath sign — Barton Cross). Follow this path down through the wood to a stile, and then cross and go for the footbridge ahead. Continue in the same direction, going up the next field to a visible stile which you cross. From here go towards the trees in front of the pebble-dash cottages ahead. Cross the stile between the trees, and follow the left-hand hedge to another stile in the hedge, opposite the end of the cottages.

Go round the front of the cottages, and follow this enclosed lane north until it reaches the metalled Barton Lane. Turn left along this until it meets Jepp's Lane at the T-junction, where again go left and cross to the lay-by. At the back corner of this is a stile, which should be crossed to follow the right-hand hedge to another stile on your right (just past a pit on the other side of the hedge). Over the stile turn left and follow the left-hand hedge until you can see a white gate in the far corner of the field. Go through the gate and follow the enclosed lane through the yard of Hoole's Farm to reach the A6.

Turn right, go over the railway bridge, cross the road and then turn left down White Horse Lane (opposite the garage).

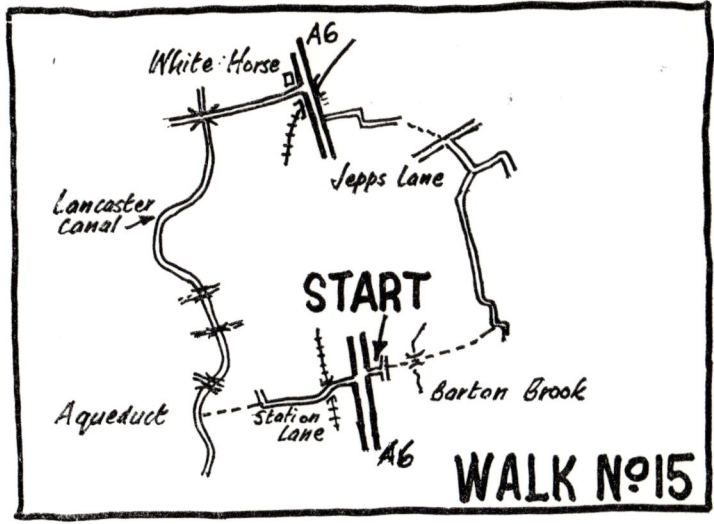

Follow the lane to the canal bridge. Go down right to the towpath, under the bridge and walk south down the canal with the water on your left. Follow the canal until the narrow wood ends a short distance after going under Bridge No. 39. Go down to the white railings and the brook is then reached by a stile.

The left-hand arch of the three-arched bridge, which carries the canal over the brook, has a planked footway. Follow this (beware of a loose plank) and then the short enclosed path that climbs slightly above the brook. Enter the field by a stile, and go up the incline to pass under the "grid" lines, making towards the houses. Cross the next field by a stile on the left of two adjacent old oaks, and follow the right-hand hedge along to a stile by a gate. This brings you to Station Lane, where a right turn will bring you back to your starting point.

Bus : *Ribble — 182 service to Woodplumpton.*

Car : *Park in the Orchard on the right past the Wheatsheaf Hotel.*

FROM THE car-park at the rear of St. Anne's church, take the path across the middle of the graveyard to a gap stile. Through this go left and follow the right-hand hedge to a stile by a gate. Cross here and again follow the right-hand hedge to another stile just short of the white farm house. Do not cross, but put your back to the stile and then cross the field to make for a corner which juts into the field. Cross the stile here and then go through the gate on your right into the next field.

From the gate go down the field, passing a clump of trees on your right, to reach a footbridge over Woodplumpton Brook. Go over the bridge and follow the brook to your right to reach a stile by a gate. Cross this and the subsequent field, heading for the farm buildings ahead. The next field is reached by crossing between an alder and oak tree. Follow parallel to the ditch on the right and go up the field to a stile by a gate. Continue in the same direction to cross the following field. When the hedge at the far side is reached turn right and follow the hedge on your left round to a gate.

To the left of a gate is a stile — cross it, then turn right, cross a plank footbridge and follow the right-hand ditch to reach the stile by a gate facing you. Head for the white house to cross the next field, go through the gap in the fencing and reach the road by a gate to the right of two garages.

Turn left on the road, cross it and go down the farm track (footpath sign — Blackleach) on the right of the white house. Before the farm, Swillbrook Lodge, is reached turn left down an enclosed green lane. Follow this gated lane until it bends left, after which an old hedge line crosses from the left. Opposite this on the right is a stile and a plank footbridge.

Cross these and go down the field parallel to the left-hand hedge. Go past the pit on your right and then join the right-hand hedge to regain a lane by a stile (and footpath sign). Turn left down the lane and then right at the junction, following this quiet Roots Lane to reach the canal. Join the canal towpath, go under the bridge (No. 30) and follow the canal with the water on your right, passing the Jolly Roger and eventually reaching bridge number 34.

Leave the canal by a stile on the nearside of the bridge, and cross the bridge to a stile by a gate. Over here follow the right-hand hedge/fence to a gate on the right-hand side of a

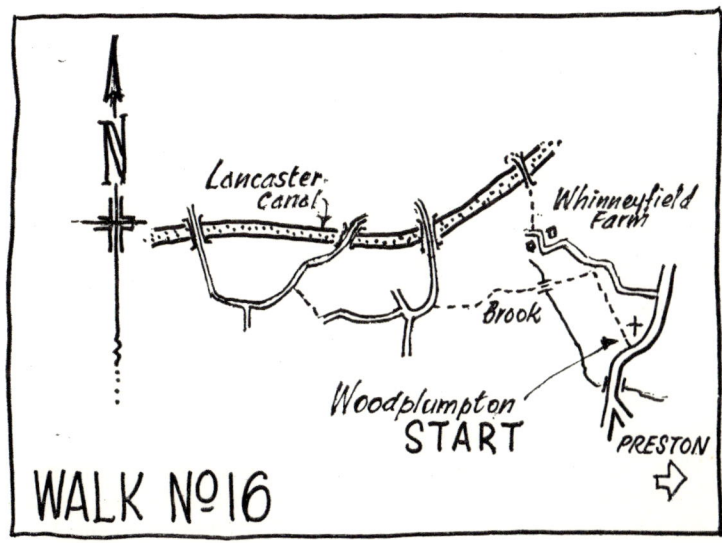

WALK Nº 16

41

farm building at Whinnyfield House. Go left into the farm-yard, through the yard and follow the farm road to Wood-plumpton.

<table>
<tr><td>17</td><td>**INGOL — WOODPLUMPTON BROOK
— LIGHTFOOT GREEN — INGOL.**</td></tr>
</table>

— 5 miles —

Bus : *P4 service to Mayfield Avenue.*

Car : *Park towards the top of Mayfield Avenue (right, off Tag Lane).*

STARTING AT Mayfield Avenue, continue round the avenue and along where it becomes a cart track by Oaktree Avenue. Continue past the Mount and Culgaith House to a stile by a gate. Cross the stile and follow the left-hand ditch and hedge to reach a gateway on your left. Cross here and follow the right-hand hedge to a stile over the ditch on your right.

From here make straight for the farm facing you — going into the yard by a stile adjacent to a gate. Then turn right and take the small gate, to the left of a white gate, to enter the field. On the left of a bulge in the right-hand corner of the field is a wooden stile by a stone gate post (between two oak trees). Cross the stile and turn left to reach another stile by a gate. Cross and follow the left-hand hedge of this narrow field for three-quarters of its length. At this stage cut diagonally right to a plank footbridge and stile in the right-hand corner of the field.

In the next field cross diagonally right to a stile by a gate. From here Lightfoot Lane is gained by going to the left, be-tween the hen cabins to a stile. Turn left on the lane, cross and then go right down a farm track that leaves opposite Ivy

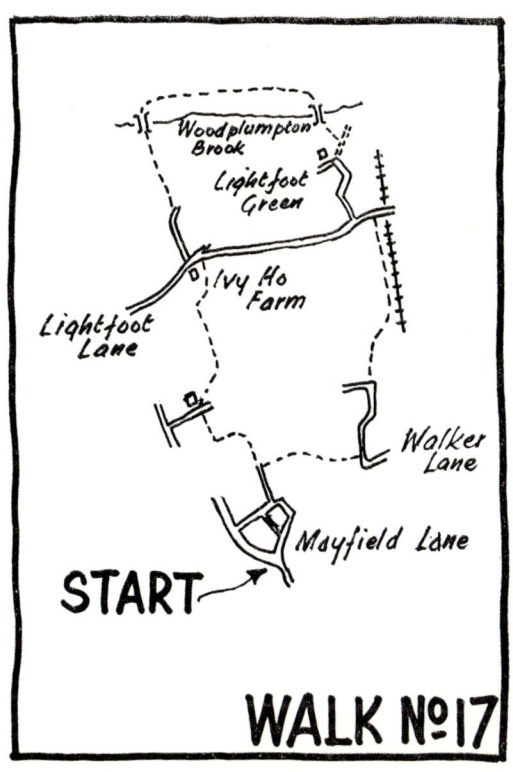

House Farm. Continue down the track until a white gate is reached on the entrance to the farmyard. A stile on the left re-admits you to the fields.

Go to cross a footbridge in the far left-hand corner of the field and when across turn right to follow the fence/hedge to another footbridge. Cross this, turn left and follow the left-hand hedge and stream down through two fields to reach Woodplumpton Brook. Cross the brook by a footbridge, turn right and keep just above the brook to a stile. Over the stile keep by the brook and then go through the gap in

43

the hedge to the next field. Continue along the brook and then make to the left-hand side of a pylon to find a stile in the corner of the field.

Cross and go below the pylon to reach a stile by the right-hand corner of the field and just above a meander in the brook. Cross and follow the left-hand fence to an access road. The land here was originally a poultry farm but is now overgrown in many places. Cross the access road and continue along the left-hand fence to a gap in the shrubs. Through the gap go to the right-hand corner, by the brook, of the next field, to reach another access road by a bricked well. Cross directly to another bricked well and again cross the field to the far right-hand corner by the brook. Go over the fence and follow the brook along to a footbridge.

Cross the brook here and go straight up the fenced path to reach an access road by a large shed. Go over the concrete at the front of the shed and follow the path by the left-hand fence to a rough track. Then turn right and go along to reach a metalled road in front of the farmhouse. Turn left here and follow this to Lightfoot Lane, ignoring the various side tracks.

At this lane, cross and turn left to reach a stile by the corner of the railway bridge (footpath sign — Walker Lane and Stour Lodge). Cross the stile and follow the railside fence until it eventually leads down to a footbridge. Over the bridge turn right over a stile, and follow the stream (on your right) through two fields to reach a stile by some farm buildings. Over this stile turn right and then left up Walker Lane, continuing until a driveway leaves on the right by a white gate.

Just after this is a stile (footpath sign — Mayfield Avenue). Cross, and follow the right-hand hedge down over a footbridge and then along to a double stile in the far right-hand corner of the field. Cross these, turn left and follow the left-hand hedge to a stile and gate. Over the stile retrace your steps along Mayfield Avenue.

Bus : *P1 service to Lane Ends or P3 service to top of Waterloo Road, then walk to Haslem Park.*

Car : *Park outside the entrance to Haslem Park, off Blackpool Road.*

STARTING IN Haslem Park, go round by the tennis courts and along to the bridge over Savick Brook, a couple of hundred yards to the left of the duck pond. Cross this, go through the gate and follow the distinct path to reach the canal. Go down to the canal towpath and follow it along, with the canal on your right, eventually reaching Bridge No. 18 at Lea Road. Go up on to the road, over the bridge to cross the canal and along the road to a stile on the right after the stone cross (footpath sign — Cottam; Hoyles Lane).

Over the stile go to another stile by a gate in the far right-hand corner of the field. Over this turn left and follow the fence to a stile in the far left-hand corner. Cross this and continue in same direction (with a right-hand ditch and hedge) to reach a stile in the top left-hand corner of the field. Cross this, the path going between two pits, to reach Hoyle's Lane via an enclosed path on the right of the farm. Turn right on the lane and cross to a gate on your left (footpath sign — Lower Bartle).

Go across the field to a plank footbridge near a gate (in a line with the farm on your left) crossing and continuing along the side of a small depression to a stile. Over the stile follow the left-hand hedge to a gate in the far left-hand corner of the field. Through the gate turn right down an enclosed lane that leads into a field. Continue to follow the left-hand hedge until you come to a stile in the furthermost corner

45

facing a white farmhouse. Over the stile turn right and follow the right-hand hedge to two green gates in the far right-hand corner of the field. A stile by the left-hand gate is crossed to follow the left-hand fence to a stile and footbridge.

Over the footbridge go to reach Hoyles Lane by a gate between the bungalow and house facing you. Cross straight over and go down the short lane to reach two adjacent farm tracks where this lane bends left. Take the right-hand of these two (footpath sign — Lea Road and Canal), bearing left to pass between the two farms (Woodfield and Cottam Lodge). Continue down the enclosed lane to reach the canal at Valentine House Farm, following the track until it leads you up to the towpath.

Leave the canal at bridge No. 16. Turn right to go down Cottam Lane, and follow this until it is crossed by the railway. Some steps and a gate to your left, on the near side of the bridge, lead you again into Haslem Park.

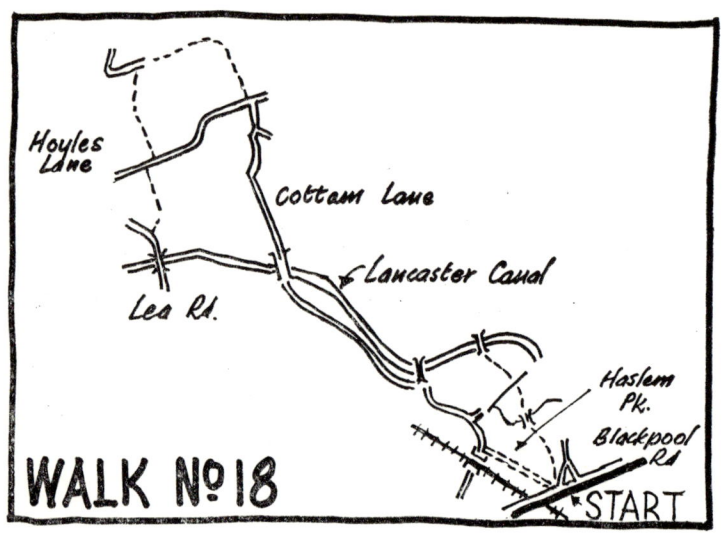

Bus: *Preston Corporation — P3 to Tudor Avenue.*

Car: *Tudor Avenue, Lea, right, off Blackpool Road.*

GO DOWN Tudor Avenue to reach the bridge over Savick Brook. Turn left on the track before the bridge and follow the brook by the playing fields to reach a tubular iron foot-bridge which you cross. Continue along the stream, this time on your left, until you have to turn right at the far corner of the golf-course. A short distance brings you to a wooden footbridge, which is crossed. From here follow the left-hand fence to a stile and over this follow the path uphill to the left of two pylons.

A stile by the pylon leads you into the next field. Follow the right-hand hedge to a stile by a gate, and over it turn left into "Back Lane." Follow the tarmacadam lane past the bungalow and farm on your right until the second left-hand bend — just short of a bungalow with a red-tiled roof. On your right, on the bend, is a stile between two gates (footpath sign — Lea Town). Cross the stile and follow the left-hand hedge to a gate, through which a stile and footbridge (by another gate) are on your left.

Cross these and turn right to follow the right-hand hedge to another stile and gate. Cross and go along the enclosed path to reach the road at Lea Town. Go right, and after the end of the bungalows, on the left-hand side of the road are two gates — an iron one and a white one. Continue past these until you come to a stile, hidden in the left-hand hedge, opposite a farmyard (footpath sign — Lea Lane). Go straight across the field, keeping the pit to your right, and round the back of the pit follow the left-hand fence and hedge to a stile in the corner.

47

Over the stile, go across to the white gate next to Mason House Farm. Through the gate, go past the farm and along the track to Lea Lane. Turn right on the lane, passing over the railway bridge to join the canal towpath by the next bridge. Go along the towpath, with the canal on your right, eventually reaching bridge No. 16.

Leave the canal here, going down the track to the right (Cottam Lane) until it crosses Savick Brook. Over the bridge turn sharp right and follow the path along the brook, under the railway and below the bungalows and housing estate, keeping the school to your left (brook still on right) to reach Ainsdale Drive at the bottom of Savick Estate. Go along to reach Lea Road which you cross to a stile (footpath sign — Lea Town). Over the stile continue with the brook on your right to a gate on the far side of the field. Through this you reach Tudor Avenue and your starting point.

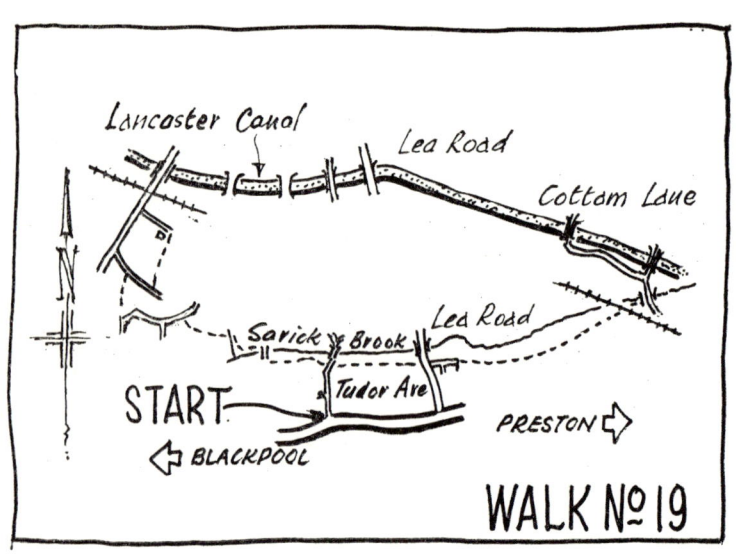

SCALES — TREALES — BOLTON CROFT — SALWICK — SCALES.

— 6 miles —

Bus : Ribble — Kirkham and Blackpool services to School Lane, Newton with Scales.

Car : Park down Vicarage Lane, right, off Blackpool Road.

FROM Scales go down Vicarage Lane, passing the village hall on the left and the right turn to Clifton to reach where the lane turns sharp left just after East View Farm. Go round the bend and halfway between the corner and Moor Farm is a gap (stile) in the right-hand hedge. Go across, enter the field and make for the gate facing you. Through the gate follow the field right down to its bottom most right-hand corner (it is an irregular shaped field with three right-hand corners — use the white, sail-less windmill as a guide).

Cross the stile and ditch to the right and turn to follow the left-hand hedge and fence down to the ditch. Turn left and follow the ditch to a footbridge, crossing to go up to the railway fence. Follow the fence left to reach a farm access bridge over the railway. Go over and make for the brick barn slightly to your right across the field, a gate on the left admitting you to the farmyard. Through the yard you come to a lane on which you turn left.

Go on the right-hand side of the lane and turn right up the track to the white Treales windmill. Adjacent to the gate of the windmill is a stone stile on your right — cross this and the wooden stile at the end of the wall. From here follow the left-hand hedge round until it leads you to a gate and thence a narrow metalled lane. Turn right down the lane but cross the stone stile by the first gate you

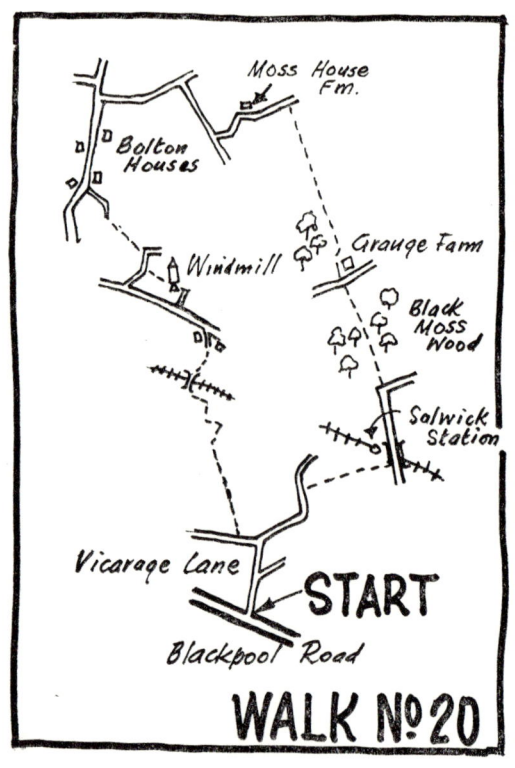

Moss House Fm.

Bolton Houses

Windmill

Grange Farm

Black Moss Wood

Salwick Station

Vicarage Lane

← START

Blackpool Road

WALK № 20

come to on your left. Then continue along the right-hand hedge to another stone stile and a series of wooden stiles — keeping the hedge on your right — to reach a short enclosed lane that brings you on to the road by the hamlet of Bolton Houses. Turn right on the road through the hamlet, and then right again onto a narrow lane. Take the first right along the lane and follow it until you come to a left turn. Go left here, passing Moss House Farm to come to a point where a long wood and ditch reach the road from the left — just short of Stanley Grange Farm. Here you leave the road by a stile on your right. Follow the left-hand hedge up through two fields and cross over the ditch at the top corner of the second field. Over the stile continue in the same direction, passing between two pits to reach the left-hand corner of Livesey Wood. Follow the side of the wood to the far left-hand corner and then go to meet the road by a stile — with Grange Farm over to your left.

Cross the lane to a small swing gate; through this follow the left-hand hedge through two fields to reach Black Moss Wood. The short path across the wood to a small gate is obvious. From the gate aim for the railway bridge — to the left of Salwick station — which will lead you to a stile by a gate. Over the stile follow the road to cross the railway, and immediately over the bridge turn right to go down the concrete steps.

Continue by the rail-side fence to reach a stile where an iron swing gate used to be. Over the stile make for the gate on the immediate left of the wood facing you, and then follow the track under the pylons. Carry straight on to a small swing gate — half way between the white bungalow and Dingle Farm — and through this follow the farm lane to the left to reach Vicarage Lane. Retrace the lane to your start.

SPONSORED WALK ROUTE A. — 13 miles —

PENWORTHAM BRIDGE — RIVER RIBBLE — HUTTON — LOWER PENWORTHAM.

Bus : *Preston Corporation — Broadgate services to Penwortham Bridge.*

Car : *Park by riverside road to Power Station.*

FROM Penwortham Bridge follow the western bank (the Penwortham side) of the river Ribble down stream past the power station. Continue along the riverside track that passes opposite the entrance to Preston Dock for approximately four miles. This brings you to a small sewerage station and to where the embankment sweeps away from the river. Follow the embankment until a metal trough appears down on your left. Cross the stile by the trough and follow the left-hand fence to a gate at the end of Grange Lane. Go through the gate towards Old Grange Farm.

Just short of the farm a gate on your left stands opposite one on your right. Go through that on your left, and follow the line of trees until you are opposite the edge of the farm buildings on the right. Turn right and skirt these buildings to a gate opposite a bungalow, through which turn left along Grange Lane. Continue along the lane, turning right at the first junction and then left into Ratten Lane. Follow the lane until, after a series of bends, a footpath leaves on the left opposite the farm cottages "Collingwood" and "Ellersley" (No. 57). It passes through a stile and follows down the field a groove which runs parallel to the hedges. At the bottom of the field cross the stile, and then the wooden bridge below.

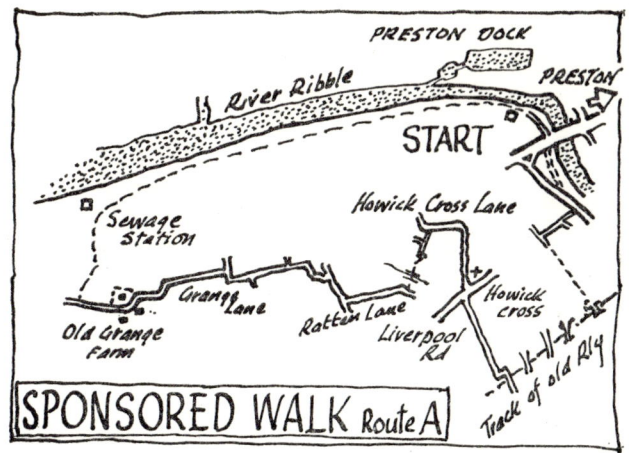

SPONSORED WALK Route A

bridge, crossing this to follow the left-hand hedge to a gate.
bridge, crossing this to follow the left-hand edge to a gate.
Go through the gate and follow the enclosed lane to reach a
metalled road, continuing straight down this road to a T-
junction just after Marigold Cottage. Turn right into
Howick Cross Lane, and follow the metalled road to reach
Liverpool Road at Howick Cross. Cross over to Howick
Moor Lane, slightly to the right, and follow down the lane,
continuing straight ahead when the metalled section ends
(footpath sign — Broad Oak Lane).

By the gate at the end a narrow path winds off to the left.
This path, in a narrow wood, leads to the trackway of the
disused Preston/Southport railway line. Turn left along
this, going through the Broad Oak Lane level crossing and
under two stone-arched bridges to reach the metal bridge.
Climb out from the cutting to the left of the bridge where
there is a stile by a wooden fence.

Cross the stile and follow the green path to a white gate
and stile. Thirty yards after this turn right (Bridlepath
sign) and follow the track down to Leyland Road. Turn

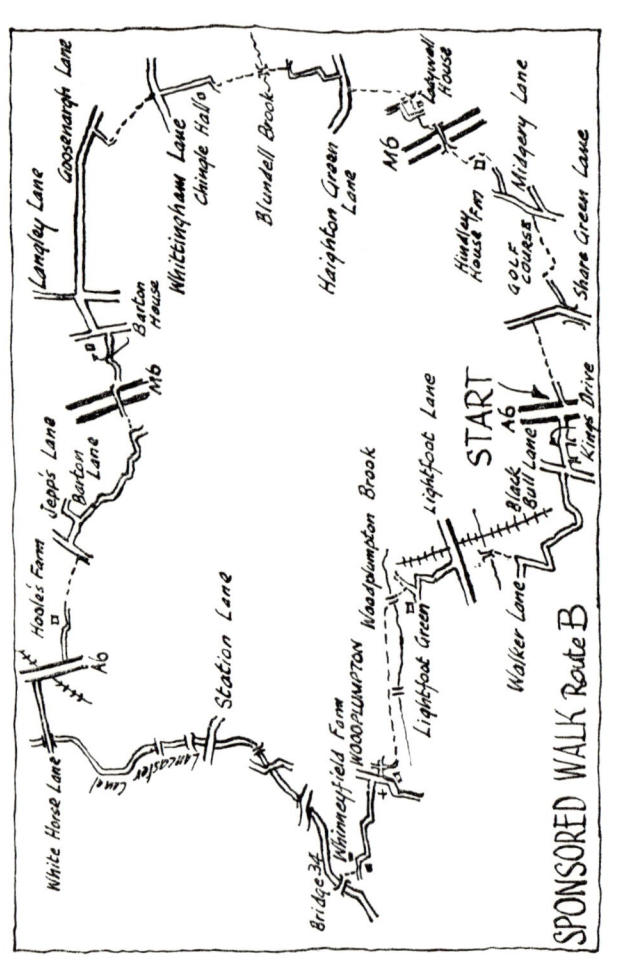

SPONSORED WALK Route B

right and cross the road, then go left along the river bank to reach Penwortham Bridge, with Penwortham Holme playing fields on your left.

SPONSORED WALK ROUTE B. — 14 miles —

FULWOOD — HAIGHTON — GOOSNARGH — BARTON — WOODPLUMPTON — FULWOOD.

Bus : *Garstang, Morecambe, P2 services to St. Vincent's Road.*

Car : *Park down St. Vincent's Road.*

FOLLOW THE enclosed pathway which is a continuation of St. Vincent's Road until Sharoe Green Lane is reached, where turn right and go down towards the brook bridge. Just before the bridge turn left over a stile (footpath sign — Midgery Lane) and follow the path along the brookside and over the bridge. Continue along the path across the golf course and then along the right-hand hedge of one field to Midgery Lane. Turn left down the lane until you cross the bridge.

Turn up the steep farm road to the right, and after passing Hindley Hill Farm on your left, you reach Hindley House Farm. Incline right as you enter the farmyard and go by the side of the farm buildings to join the fields by a gate. From here you will see a footbridge which carries the path over the motorway; to reach it keep to the left-hand hedge until you are at a point opposite. Cross over the motorway by this bridge, and then bear left and cross over a stile on the right in the corner of the field. Follow the left-hand hedge to join the lane by Ladywell House, St. Mary's well being a few yards to the right in front of the house.

Go straight across the lane to a stile by the side of the house, and follow the right-hand hedge to a farm road with a stone stile opposite. Beyond this stile keep by the right-hand hedge through three fields, crossing the stone stile on the right of two trees and reaching the road by a long narrow field. Turn right along the road and pass a house with a monkey tree in the garden on your way to a lane on the left. Follow this lane until you reach a stile by the second right-hand bend. Cross this and go diagonally to a stile in the far corner of the field.

In the next field incline left to cross Blundell Brook by a wooden footbridge, and then climb the rise to a stile on the right of a crab-apple tree. Cross over and follow the right-hand hedge to join a lane that leads through Chingle Hall Farm and Chingle House to Whittingham Lane. Go a few yards to the right to a stone stile on the opposite side of the road. Through this follow the left-hand hedge to the next stile, and then the right-hand hedge until it reaches a track that leads to Goosnargh Lane. Turn left and follow the lane for approximately three-quarters of a mile to a T-junction with Langley Lane.

Cross the road and go down the private road to Barton House, turning left at the house along the lane to follow the surfaced lane to the right through a metal gate. At its end continue along the right-hand hedge to a motorway foot-bridge. Go over the bridge and stile and follow the right-hand hedge to a stile by a metal gate into a lane. Turn right and follow the enclosed lane north until it reaches the metalled Barton Lane, where turn left to meet Jepp's Lane at the T-junction.

Turn left and cross to the lay-by, at the back corner of which is a stile. Cross this and follow the right-hand hedge to a stile on your right (just past a pit on the other side of the hedge). Over the stile turn left and follow the left-hand hedge until you can see a white gate in the far corner of the field. Go through the gate and follow the enclosed lane through the yard of Hoole's Farm to reach the A6. Turn right, go over the railway bridge, cross the road and then turn left down White Horse Lane (opposite the garage).

Follow the lane to the canal bridge, going down right to the towpath, under the bridge and walking south down the canal (with the water on your left). Continue on the towpath for approximately $2\frac{1}{2}$ miles until Bridge 34 is reached. Leave the canal by a stile on the far side of the bridge, crossing the bridge to a stile by a gate. Over here follow the right-hand hedge/fence to reach a gate on the right-hand side of a farm building at Whinnyfield House. Go left into the farmyard, through the yard and follow the farm road to Woodplumpton.

On entering Woodplumpton go right towards the village, then turn left into the Orchard (just before the Wheatsheaf Hotel). At the end of the houses turn right and go down the enclosed path — ignore the first left turn — to bear left and down to Woodplumpton Brook. Turn left and follow the brook to a footbridge — do not cross but continue along the brook to a stile. Over this keep by the brook and then go through the gap in the hedge to the next field. Continue along the brook and then make to the left-hand side of a pylon to find a stile in the corner of the field.

Cross and go below the pylon to reach a stile by the right-hand corner of the field and just above a meander in the brook. Then follow the left-hand fence to an access road — the land here was originally a poultry farm but is now overgrown in many places. Cross the access road and continue along the left-hand fence to a gap in the shrubs. Through this go to the right-hand corner, by the brook, of the next field to reach another access road by a bricked well. Go directly to another bricked well and again cross the field to the far right-hand corner by the brook. Cross the fence and follow the brook along to a footbridge.

Go over the brook here and straight up the fenced path to reach an access road by a large shed. Go over the concrete at the front of the shed and follow the path by the left-hand fence to a rough track. When this is reached turn right and

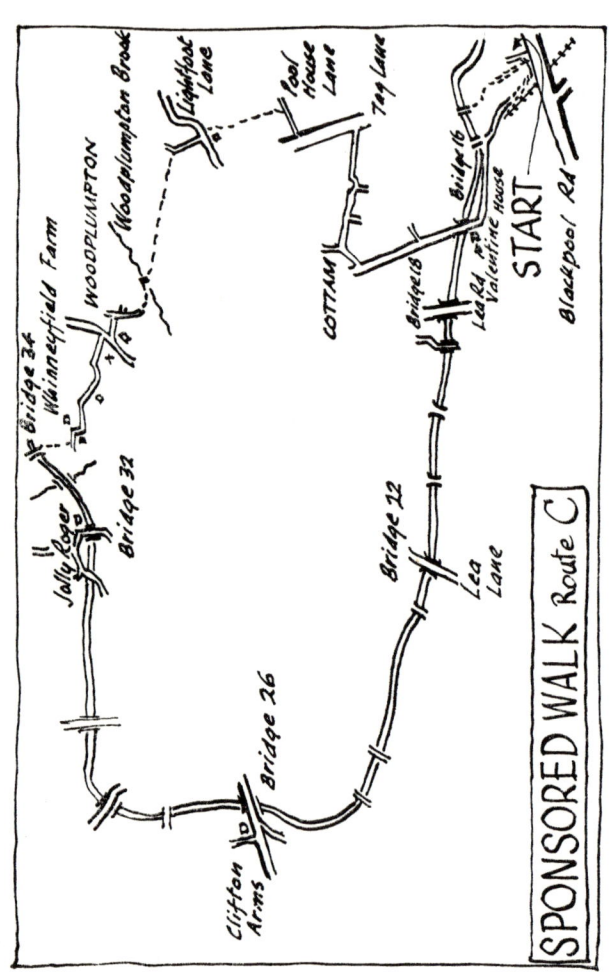

SPONSORED WALK Route C

Jolly Roger
Bridge 34
Whinneyfield Farm
Bridge 32
WOODPLUMPTON
Woodplumpton Brook
Lightfoot Lane
Pool House Lane
Tag Lane
Bridge 26
Clifton Arms
Bridge 12
Lea Lane
COTTAM
Bridge 18
Lea Ld Rd
Valentine House
Bridge 16
START
Blackpool Rd

go along to a metalled road in front of the farm house. Turn left here and follow this to reach Lightfoot Lane, ignoring the various side tracks. At the lane cross and turn left to come to a stile by the corner of the railway bridge (footpath sign — Walker Lane and Stour Lodge).

Cross the stile and follow the railside fence until it eventually leads down to a footbridge. Over the bridge turn right over a stile, and follow the stream (on your right) through two fields to reach a stile by some farm buildings. Over this turn right, and then left up Walker Lane. Continue along the lane until, on a sharp left-hand bend, it becomes Boys Lane, crosses over the railway and reaches the junction with Black Bull Lane. Cross over the road into Kings Drive and follow to the A6 and your starting point.

SPONSORED WALK ROUTE C. — 13 miles —

HASLEM PARK — WOODPLUMPTON — COTTAM — HASLEM PARK.

Bus : *P1 service to Lane Ends or P3 service to top of Waterloo Road, then walk to Haslem Park.*

Car : *Park outside the entrance to Haslem Park, off Blackpool Road.*

STARTING IN Haslem Park, go round by the tennis courts and along to the bridge over Savick Brook, a couple of hundred yards to the left of the duck pond. Cross this, go through the gate and follow the distinct path to reach the canal. Go down to the canal towpath and follow it, with the canal on your right, for approximately seven miles.

At Bridge No. 34 leave the canal by a stile on the nearside, crossing the bridge to a stile by a gate. Over here follow the right-hand hedge/fence to reach a gate on the right-hand side of a farm building at Whinnyfield House. Go left into the farmyard, through the yard and follow the farm road to Woodplumpton. On entering Woodplumpton go right towards the village, then turn left into the Orchard (just before the Wheatsheaf Hotel). At the end of the houses turn right and go down the enclosed path — ignore the first left turn — to bear left and down to Woodplumpton Brook.

Turn left and follow the brook to a footbridge. Cross the bridge and go straight on, with a high hedge on your right, to a stile in the right-hand corner of the field. Over the stile follow the right-hand hedge of a larger field, at the corner of which cross a stile and a footbridge. Turn sharp left and cross a small field to a further stile and footbridge, going over the bridge to turn right towards the farm. Pass through a gap in the rails to the right of the farm and make for a stile in the right-hand corner of the field.

Over the stile turn right and follow the farm road to Lightfoot Lane. Turn left for a short distance and cross the road to a stile (footpath sign — Pool House Lane). Over this go down the field parallel to the left-hand fence/hedge to meet a stile on your right (by a gate). Cross and go diagonally left across the field to a stile and plank foot-bridge in the far corner. Then aim for a gate and stile in the far right-hand corner of the next field. Cross the stile and follow the right-hand hedge to a stile by a stone gate post. Over this go to a small gate in the left-hand corner of the field by the farm buildings.

Go along Pool House Lane to reach Tag Lane, where turn left along the pavement for a short distance (less than ¼ mile). Cross the road and turn right into Cottam Hall Lane to reach Cottam Hall Farm where the track goes right and becomes a metalled road. Continue along the lane until it bends sharp right (footpath sign — Lea Road and Canal). Bear left to pass between the two farms (Woodfield and Cottam Lodge).

Continue down the enclosed lane to reach the canal at Valentine House Farm. Follow this track and it will lead you up to the canal towpath, which should be left, at Bridge

No. 16. Turn right to go down Cottam Lane, and follow this until it is crossed by the railway. Some steps and a gate on your left, on the near side of the bridge, lead you again into Haslem Park.

The Canal Bridge, Lea Road (see Walk 18).

LOG OF WALKS

Number	Miles	Date	Notes
1			
2			
3			
4			
5			
6			
7			
8			
9			
10			
11			
12			

LOG OF WALKS

Number	Miles	Date	Notes
13			
14			
15			
16			
17			
18			
19			
20			
A			
B			
C			

THE COUNTRY CODE.

Guard against all risk of fire

Fasten all gates

Keep dogs under proper control

Keep to the paths

Avoid damaging fences, hedges and walls

Leave no litter

Safeguard water supplies

Protect wild life, wild plants and trees

Go carefully on roads

Respect the life of the countryside